Original title:
Mango Madness

Copyright © 2025 Creative Arts Management OÜ
All rights reserved.

Author: Sophia Kingsley
ISBN HARDBACK: 978-1-80586-374-8
ISBN PAPERBACK: 978-1-80586-846-0

Pulped Delight in Every Bite

In the kitchen, a dance so bright,
Juicy splatters, what a sight!
Peeling joy, giggles arise,
Sticky fingers, oh what a prize!

With every munch, we all agree,
This fruity treasure's wild and free.
Chasing drips like kids at play,
Parting smiles at the end of the day.

Serenade of the Swaying Trees

Listen close, the trees do sway,
Whisper songs of a sunny day.
Fruity whispers in the breeze,
Bouncing laughter, oh if you please!

A cheeky parrot joins the fun,
Chattering tales till the day is done.
Nature's jest, a colorful tease,
Swinging branches, dancing leaves.

Vortex of Fruity Temptation

Round and round, we spin in zest,
Caught in a fruity, wild quest.
Juicy joy is hard to resist,
A whirlwind of flavor, can't be missed!

Falling slices, a tasty whirl,
Bursting sweetness gives a twirl.
Giggles follow each tasty bite,
A carnival feast, pure delight!

Vibrant Hues of the Palate

Colors splash on every plate,
A canvas of flavor, feeling great.
Golden orange, bright and bold,
Tales of laughter, sweet and told!

Slicing smiles, we gather 'round,
With each taste, joy can be found.
A zesty giggle, a playful tease,
Beneath the trees, where fruits appease.

Tasting the Tropics

In the market, yellow dreams,
A fruit that giggles and beams,
Splashing juice on cheeky grins,
Eating slices, laughter spins.

Sticky fingers, oh what fun,
Under the bright, blazing sun,
Unruly bites, a tasty spree,
Sipping smoothies, wild and free.

Fruity Fantasia

A slice takes flight, quite absurd,
It dances, flits, and sings a word,
Chasing kids in playful jest,
Swirling flavors, oh so blessed.

Peel it fast, don't let it hide,
It's a party on the slide,
What's that flavor? Sweet surprise!
With each bite, the laughter flies.

Sweet Temptation's Dance

Twist and twirl, the fruit declares,
A juicy jig that no one cares,
Sticky sweet on a summer day,
Bursting joy, come join the play!

Bouncing bowls, a fruity feast,
Dripping joy, a sticky beast,
Round and round, we cheer and prance,
All partake in this wild dance.

Beneath the Canopy of Flavor

Under trees, a shady nook,
A treasure trove to gladly look,
Gather friends for snacks galore,
Pitter-patter, who wants more?

Slick with syrup, smiles so wide,
Watch them bounce, we laugh and glide,
Floating dreams in every bite,
A fruit-filled frenzy, pure delight!

Sweetness Stolen in the Shade

In the heat, I found a treat,
A yellow orb, that's hard to beat.
A squirrel dashed by with a grin,
It snatched my prize; oh, where to begin?

My sticky hands, my goofy dance,
I took a bite, oh what a chance!
But bees arrived for a taste too,
I waved them off, quite like a fool!

Lush Canopy of Cravings

Under leafy shades so wide,
I sat and dreamed with my wormy side.
Fruits above swayed with delight,
Mischief brewed; I'd take a bite!

My friend tripped over a branch, oh dear!
He tumbled down, gave a loud cheer.
Laughter echoed, sweet and ripe,
As juicy drips ran down like hype!

Kissed by the Tropics

In a land where sunshine beams,
I chased my dreams with fruity schemes.
A fellow shouted, "Catch that flare!"
But my foot slipped—what a wild affair!

The nectar splashed like a silly scene,
On a bright shirt—now a sticky sheen!
We danced around in fruity bliss,
Who knew that juice could feel like this?

Tales of Ripeness and Revelry

Gather 'round, I've tales to share,
Of sticky fingers and fruity air.
We climbed the tree, we reached the prize,
But lost our grip—oh, what a surprise!

The fruits fell down like laughter's sound,
As we rolled on the grass, joy unbound.
Sweet stains upon our jubilant frowns,
Capers of sweetness in our clowning gowns!

Sun-Drenched Delights

In the sun they sit, oh so bright,
Golden orbs of pure delight.
Tongue out, I take a big bite,
Juices flowing, what a sight!

Sticky fingers, laughter fills the air,
Tasting joy, and without a care.
Neighbors peek, their faces bare,
As I dance in fruity flair!

Juicy Inspirations

Curved like smiles, they wait in line,
Tropical treasures, pure and divine.
Creating bliss with every rhyme,
A fruit so sweet, it's simply prime!

Winding shades of sunny zest,
Nibbles shared, who feels the best?
A fruity feast, a true conquest,
In every bite, we feel so blessed!

The Poetry of Peeling

Oh, the thrill of the peel glides down,
Flesh revealed in this sticky brown.
With every twist, I'm lost, I drown,
In this weird fruit-loving town!

Worn-out shirts, the stains won't fade,
But happiness is freshly made.
Laughter echoes, joy cascades,
As the fruits perform their parade!

Sunlit Harvests

Bobbing in bowls, they shine so bright,
Slicing, dicing, what a sight!
The laughter rings, pure delight,
As fruity wonders take their flight!

Throwing pits like little stars,
Cheering crowds from near and far.
In the sunlight, we raise the bars,
Living joy with fruit-filled jars!

Tropical Whispers in the Breeze

In a land where fruits do prance,
The juicy trees begin to dance.
With laughter spilling all around,
Bright cheeks and sticky joy abound.

A tumble here, a slip right there,
Oh what fun we have, I swear!
Our joyful feast, a slippery race,
As laughter hangs in every place.

Golden globes that tease the sun,
We dive right in, oh what a run!
In every bite, a giggle hides,
Sweet madness bursts and joy collides.

The Juicy Calamity

The fruit fell hard from way up high,
A comical, unexpected fly!
It splattered wide, a fruity ballet,
With laughter ringing, come what may.

We slipped and slid upon the floor,
Who knew fruit could make us roar?
With sticky hands and smiling grins,
The juiciness makes us all kin.

In every pit, a story lies,
Of giggling friends and fruit-filled skies.
A tasty mess, our shared delight,
In this calamity, all feels right.

Paradise Found in Every Slice

A golden slice, oh what a cheer,
We gather 'round, it's time to steer.
With every cut, a sweet surprise,
Unexpected joy that never lies.

We toss the seeds like little stars,
Aiming high for fruit-filled bars.
The juice drips down, we laugh so loud,
In fruity glory, we are proud.

Each slice unveils a tropical song,
A melody where we all belong.
In fruity bites, the world feels wide,
With sunshine smiles, we take the ride.

Sun-Drenched Euphoria

Underneath the blazing sky,
A fruit feast makes the good times fly.
With laughter bursting like the day,
We savor joy in every way.

A clumsy catch, a fruity fling,
The sun-kissed joy makes our hearts sing.
With giggles shared and bites divine,
We float in sunshine, feeling fine.

Oh, what a sight, our silly crew,
With sticky hands and laughter too.
In sun-drenched moments, we unite,
In sweet escape, our hearts take flight.

The Bounty of Bliss

In a grove so bright and bold,
Laughter blooms like marigold.
Sticky fingers on a spree,
Sweet delight is wild and free.

Juicy treasures drape the trees,
Buzzing bees with playful ease.
Gentle breezes share the cheer,
Nature's joy is surely near.

Smiles burst out like bursting fruit,
Tickled souls, we dance to root.
Golden hues in summer's grasp,
We relish every tasty gasp.

What a splendid, silly chase,
Fruit-filled laughter in each place.
Joyful moments, bright and clear,
In this bounty, we draw near.

Fruitful Whispers

Whispers float among the leaves,
Tickling laughter, joy that weaves.
A plump delight, a radiant tease,
Chasing dreams with giggles and ease.

Ripe with flavor, bursting bright,
Every bite's a sheer delight.
With every drip and cheesy grin,
This fruit party makes us spin.

Oh, the tricks that fruit can play,
Rolling down the hill, hooray!
Caught in chaos, laughter flies,
Juicy moments, pure surprise.

Chortles echo in the sun,
Nature's joke, oh what fun!
In this orchard filled with cheer,
We find sweet joy each time it's near.

Orchard of Wonders

An orchard painted bright and sweet,
Where every flavor begs to meet.
Surprises hide in every bite,
As giggles dance in morning light.

A plucky fruit jumps off the tree,
Pelting friends in glee, yippee!
Socks soaked from a splashy fight,
This playful scene feels just right.

Squirrels squabble, critters cheer,
While fuzzy fruits pirouette near.
With every toss, a playful shout,
Life is rich, there's no doubt.

In this haven of pure fun,
Laughter sparkles like the sun.
In every cranny, joy abounds,
In our hearts, sweet bliss resounds.

Sunkissed Pleasure

In a sunlit world, we prance,
Dancing fruits invite romance.
Sticky smiles and laughter loud,
Nature's gifts make us so proud.

Sunkissed skins and giggly squeals,
A playful tug-o-war that feels.
Juicy drops on grassy ground,
In every bite, pure joy is found.

Chasing shadows, dodging greed,
With every jump, a fruity deed.
We stumble, wobble, then we leap,
For playful fun, we'll make a heap.

Beneath the trees of enough delight,
Our hearts soar as we take flight.
In this joyful, fruity tease,
We share our laughter with the breeze.

Paradise in Each Bite

In a sunlit orchard, joy takes flight,
With every taste, the world feels right.
Fuzzy skins and golden glow,
One sweet slice, and I'm aglow.

Dancing under the leafy shade,
In fruity bliss, my worries fade.
Laughter bubbles, mouths are stained,
Life's a feast, and I'm unchained.

Golden Hour Euphoria

As the sun dips low, the laughter grows,
Golden drops dribble from my nose.
Sipping joy from fuzzy skin,
With each bite, I fall right in.

Sticky fingers, happy grins,
Sweet surprises, where fun begins.
Sunshine laughter in the air,
Who knew fruits could bring such flair?

Ripe Adventures Await

Exploring trees like a treasure map,
Every bite, a fruity clap.
Thick and juicy, oh what luck,
My taste buds sing, they're totally struck.

A fruit fight starts, and all's fair,
Rolling peels without a care.
Laughter echoes, joy ignites,
In our sweet world of fruity delights.

Juices Flowing

Juices flowing, what a scene,
Sticky hair, I'm a fruit machine!
Slurping joy, no care at all,
In this fruity frenzy, I stand tall.

With every giggle, a bite we take,
Turning every moment, a piece of cake.
In this orchard, oh so bright,
Every drip brings pure delight.

Tasting the Golden Hour

In a grove of tossled trees,
Fruits hang like little suns,
Juicy drips with every squeeze,
Messy fun when it runs.

With sticky hands and giggles loud,
We race to catch the next sweet bite,
No worry of our parents' crowd,
A feast of joy, pure delight.

Runaway peels on the ground,
Friends chase each other with glee,
Laughter echoes all around,
In the golden glow, we're free.

Festive Flavors of the Tropics

A splash of yellow on the table,
Visions of sunrise in a bowl,
Slice, and dice, we are quite able,
A carnival for every soul.

Ice cream drips on summer days,
Sticky smiles as we unite,
Dancing with the syrupy rays,
Such fruity joy feels so right.

Jam spills over with a cheer,
Spread it wide, don't be discreet,
Every taste brings a new cheer,
Tropical vibes cannot be beat.

Ripening Romance

Underneath the stars' sweet gaze,
A picnic spread with laughter bright,
Fruits are ripe in twilight's haze,
For two, the world feels just right.

Giggling as we share a slice,
Juicy bites that make us grin,
Each laugh echoes, oh so nice,
In every taste, love can begin.

Sticky fingers, hearts that race,
Sunset paints the sky with flair,
In this fruity, sweet embrace,
We find magic in the air.

Dancing with Sunshine

Two left feet on the dance floor,
A rhythm that makes all eyes bright,
Swirling with fruit, oh what a score,
A golden twirl in the light.

With each spin, the laughter grows,
Falling down in fits of joy,
The beat, sweet as summer's prose,
Dance like a carefree girl or boy.

Step by step, we share a cheer,
Juicy treats thrown all around,
While the sun melts slowly near,
In this moment, love is found.

Palate Paradise

In the market, colors collide,
Yellow orbs, with smiles so wide.
I took a bite, juice on my chin,
Tangled in sweetness, where do I begin?

Bouncing around, they roll like balls,
Fruits in the air, watch how they fall!
Lemonade dreams in a bright glass moat,
Chasing my buddy, the slippery boat.

Sticky fingers, a sticky face,
In this fruit game, I've found my place.
A treasure trove of flavor and fun,
Let's savor the laughs, we've just begun!

A party in the park, everyone's there,
Splat! A fruit toss, a wild affair.
With giggles and grins under sunny skies,
Sweet laughter echoes beneath the rise.

The Essence of Sunlit Fruit

Behold the golden, they wink and sway,
Dancing in sunlight, come out to play!
I slip on juice, now I'm on a spree,
A zesty adventure, just me and my glee.

Chasing down dreams, they lure me close,
A fragrant festival, I love them most.
Wobbling treats in a sticky embrace,
Each bite's a riot, a laugh, a race.

Belly flops in flavor, I take a dive,
What joy to feel so very alive!
Comedic crunch in each squishy bite,
I'm rolling with laughter, oh what a sight!

Back in the swing, I'm ready for more,
These sunlit gems leave me wanting the score.
With rib-tickling flavors, I'll shout and sing,
In this fruit fiesta, joy is the king!

The Sweetness of Tomorrow

Caught in a dream of sugary haze,
Tomorrow's sweetness winks and plays.
A mischievous sprinkle on my toast,
I'll raise a toast to what I love most!

Tropical bursts on a summer day,
A slippery slide—I'm lost in the fray.
Swirling in flavors, I'm high on delight,
A silly grin on my face, what a sight!

I barter with fruit for a moment's cheer,
No such thing as too much, my dear!
Splat! All over—oh, what a scene,
This banquet of laughter, so sweet, so green.

Tomorrow's treasure is ready to share,
In this world of fruit, love fills the air.
With chuckles and bites, we savor the swirl,
Each sticky joy is a giggling whirl.

Sunkissed Fruits Unveiled

Underneath the sun, they glow so bright,
Fruits with charm, a comedic sight.
I wipe my brow, a juice waterfall,
In this fruity world, I'm having a ball!

Giggles erupt with each zesty pop,
Slipping on sweetness, I just can't stop.
A fruit at the party is always divine,
Laughter and mess, oh how they entwine!

Beneath the trees, the laughter erupts,
With every soft nudge, everyone jumps!
A playful chaos, colors collide,
In this feast of flavors, I giggle and hide.

Reveling in joy as the day stretches wide,
These sunkissed treats are my favorite ride.
With fruity romance, life feels so bright,
In our comedy of flavors, we take flight!

Cascades of Citrus Bliss

In orchards bright, I leap and prance,
A yellow treasure sparks a dance.
With laughter bubbling, joy like juice,
In every bite, my mind's let loose.

Sticky fingers, oh what a sight,
Sipping sunshine, pure delight.
The tree's my friend, it swings and sways,
I giggle with it through sunny days.

Sun-Kissed Whirlwinds

A fruit so ripe, it makes me grin,
Tumbling down, it's a fruity spin.
Bouncing around the grassy floor,
With every sip, I shout for more!

Sunshine drops from branches high,
Chasing dreams that float up to the sky.
I trip and tumble in pure glee,
Nature's dance, just you and me.

Harvesting Laughter and Memories

Skins of gold and hearts so sweet,
Joyful chaos at my tiny feet.
We gather treasures, laughter bursts,
Each moment savored, oh how it thirsts!

Pits like marbles, we toss and play,
Chasing giggles the whole day.
In every bite, a memory swells,
A banquet of giggles, sweet taste smells.

Nectar's Unruly Embrace

The nectar spills, a sticky hug,
In my hair, oh what a bug!
Ridiculous antics spill from my lips,
With every drop, I take wild trips.

Splat and splurge, it's a juicy fight,
While fruit drops down, we spark delight.
With silly faces, we take a stand,
A comical feast, all so unplanned.

Essence of Sunshine on the Skin

Oh, the yellow sphere, quite a treat,
Happiness grows with each juicy bite.
Its sticky sweetness, a puzzle to test,
Laughing erupts in this fruit-loving fest.

Under the tree, giggles do flow,
Sticky hands waving, oh what a show!
Nature's gold drips from grinning faces,
A comical course of fruity embraces.

Chasing the birds, we dodge the bees,
Fumbling with cuttings, all sticky knees.
With laughter echoing through the air,
Who knew this fruit could create such flair?

As the sun sets, we smile and cheer,
Belly full, no room for fear.
With each slice, the fun multiplies,
Essence of sunshine, a fruity surprise!

Juiced Up Joys of Nature

Sippin' sunshine from a cup, oh so bright,
Giggling uncontrollably, pure delight.
Straws dancing wildly in a fray,
Who knew juice could lead to such play?

A splash here, a tint of yellow there,
The floor's a canvas, stickiness everywhere.
Chasing each drop with a laugh and a jump,
This bubbling chaos is quite the thump!

Fruits in our hair and juice on our shirts,
The neighborhood is laughing, oh what flirts!
In this juicy romp, we feel alive,
Joy in every sip, oh how we thrive!

Under the sun, we're wild and free,
Raucous laughter drifts like the breeze.
Each cup raised high, a toast we make,
Juiced up joys, for goodness' sake!

Splashes of Radiance and Flavor

Colorful splashes on a picnic spread,
Laughter erupts, with crumbs to shed.
Fruits come tumbling in a grand parade,
Who knew a bite could lead to escapade?

Hitting each other with juicy douse,
Wiping our faces like a hairy mouse.
Giggles unravel with every squeeze,
Flavor explosions bring us to our knees.

Rolling on grass, we laugh till we cry,
Feeling the sunshine and tasting the sky.
Each morsel a spark of blissful fun,
In this wacky world, we've truly won!

Hours in chaos, a sticky affair,
Playgrounds of laughter, we haven't a care.
In splashes of flavor, joy does loom,
Let's celebrate life in this fruity bloom!

Bounty of the Mischievous Sun

From the sun's grin, our treasure is found,
Twinkling laughter gathers all around.
Fruits flying high, dodging kids' hands,
A comedic bounty from nature's lands.

Sticky messes make quite the show,
Colorful giggles begin to flow.
Shrieks of delight as we dive for the prize,
Chasing the sweetness under bright skies.

With sandwiches stuck to our sleeves and a grin,
The sun adds laughter, a mischievous spin.
Juicy fiascoes and funny faces,
This sunny bounty brings wild embraces.

As evening falls, the fun's just begun,
Smiles all around, we've danced with the sun.
In this world of laughter, we find our way,
A bounty of joy at the end of the day!

Golden Delirium

In a sunny grove, they dance so bright,
Yellow orbs bouncing in pure delight.
With each silly grin, they wobble and sway,
A fruity fiesta, hip-hip-hooray!

Laughter erupts with each juicy bite,
Sticky fingers, oh what a sight!
The juice drips down like sweet summer rain,
Silly faces, driving us insane!

Rolling around, we taste the thrill,
In this wild whirlwind, time stands still.
Chasing the laughter, we're all in a race,
Covered in peels, it's a fruity embrace!

With friends all around, we cheer and sing,
In our festive world, it's a beautiful thing!
So hold onto the joy, let flavors collide,
In this golden realm, we take a fun ride!

Tropical Reveries Unleashed

Bouncing breezes in a silly parade,
Tropical fruits throw a grand charade.
With squishy squabbles and laughter so loud,
We're the happiest fools, oh so proud!

Sticky hair and fingers so sweet,
Dancing on sunshine, we can't take a seat.
With giggles exploding, we bounce to the beat,
Who knew that fruit could be such a treat?

In a splash of confusion, we run and we slide,
Messy with joy, it's a fun-filled ride.
The trees chuckle back, their branches a sway,
In this zany world, we simply play!

With a giggle and wiggle, we dance through the mire,
Chasing the joy like a chorus of choir.
In our tropical dreams, all worries subside,
Together in laughter, we joyfully glide!

Sunrise over Orchards

As dawn breaks bright, we stumble awake,
With bright yellow dreams, what fun we can make.
With giggles and grins, we dash in a spree,
To greet all the wonders, come dance with me!

The sun peeks through leaves, like a smile on a face,
Fruits tumble and roll in a sloppy embrace.
We chase the bright light with our goofy parade,
In this orchard of fun, we're never dismayed!

Through laughter and joy, we spin round and round,
In whirlwinds of sweetness, our glee can be found.
Tickled by breezes, we leap and we shout,
With each sunrise glimmer, there's never a doubt!

So join in the fun of our fruity delight,
With bad jokes and sillies, it feels just right.
With arms open wide, let's embrace the new day,
In this orchard of laughter, come on, let's play!

Chasing the Juice

With a splash and a giggle, we tumble and roll,
The hunt for the sweetness, it's good for the soul.
We're sticky and silly, all covered in cheer,
Chasing the juice, let's give a loud cheer!

In a quest for delight, we stumble and slide,
Fruits whispering secrets, they won't let us hide.
With every big bite, the glee starts to flow,
Our laughter like rivers begins to overflow!

The silly capers lead us round and round,
With splats and with plops, we're lost then found.
In a citrusy craze, we're dancing like mad,
In pursuit of the nectar, we're oh-so-glad!

So hold on tight as we chase down the fun,
With giggles and juice, we're never outrun.
In a messy embrace, let's dance without care,
In this fruity adventure, it's joy we declare!

Tropical Whirl

In the land where sunbeams dance,
A fruit swings low, takes a chance.
It wobbles, rolls, with cheeky glee,
Saying, "Come and laugh with me!"

Sticky fingers, giggles bright,
A splash of yellow, what a sight!
Juices drip down like summer rain,
Laughter echoes, nothing's plain.

A pit so big, it takes the stage,
This fruit's a star, it's all the rage.
With every bite, a burst of cheer,
Who knew delight could taste so dear?

So let us twirl, spin and share,
This sunny fruit, beyond compare.
In every slice, a giggle found,
In every laugh, we're mango-bound.

The Golden Fruit's Embrace

Oh golden orb, glowing bright,
You bring us joy, a pure delight.
With every bite, we close our eyes,
And dream of beaches, sunny skies.

You wriggle on the breakfast plate,
Causing smiles, you're never late.
Silly faces, squishy cheer,
Wiggly juice spreads far and near.

We wear you like a crown on heads,
A fruity feast, let's break the breads.
Where did you come from, oh so sweet?
"Not sure," you say, "but life's a treat!"

With every taste, another laugh,
You make us dance, you make us gaff.
Oh fruit of sun, embrace us tight,
In laughter we'll take flight tonight!

Juicy Reverie

In a grove where laughter grows,
Juicy dreams and sunny shows.
A fruit so plump, it wears a grin,
Causing chuckles time and again.

Stickiness, oh what a fight,
Juices splatter with pure delight.
Rolling down a cheeky smile,
For the fun, it's worth the while.

Time for a toast: to the golden glow,
Let's share a slice, have a show!
With every taste, our hearts will sing,
We're silly fools, we're fruits in spring!

So grab a slice, take a chance,
With juicy giggles, let's all dance.
In reverie, our spirits soar,
Around this fruit, forevermore.

Sunlit Orbs of Delight

Round and ripe, the sunlit treat,
Rolling forward, can't be beat.
A comical blob, plump and round,
In every bite, pure joy is found.

Tango in the afternoon,
Oh, what fun, we'll sing a tune!
Splatters happen, laughter flies,
Watch out now, watch for surprise!

These orbs of joy, they bounce and cheer,
Transforming every frown, oh dear!
With every munch, we shout hooray,
Delighted hearts, all here to play!

So gather 'round, let's share the cheer,
With sunlit fruit, let's hold it near.
In each sweet moment, we unite,
Under the glow, all feels right!

Ripe and Ready Dreams

In a grove where fruits do play,
The sun shines bright on this fine day.
A cheeky breeze begins to tease,
And it tickles sweetly through the trees.

With colors bold and flavors grand,
I chase my snack across the land.
A slippery slope, I start to slide,
For my favorite snack, I cannot hide!

I juggle fruits with all my might,
One takes a spin, oh what a sight!
It flies away, but I don't fret,
There's plenty more—I'm not done yet!

The laughter rolls, the juices flow,
With seeds of cheer in every throw.
In this garden, joy's the scheme,
Where every bite fulfills a dream.

Tropical Odyssey

Adventure calls in every bite,
As I embark on tasty flights.
The tangy zest, a bubbling cheer,
A world of flavors drawing near!

From tree to tongue, the quest is clear,
To find the fruit that brings the cheer.
A volcano of flavor, on a roller ride,
With giggles bursting, far and wide!

The golden treasure, oh so bright,
A fruity feast that feels just right.
I hear it whisper from the tree,
"Join the fun, come play with me!"

In puddles of juice, I'll gladly splash,
Transformed by this tropical bash.
A wild parade of taste awaits,
With laughter loud at fruity fates!

Juicy Journeys

Pack your bags, we're off today,
To a juicy world where fruit can play.
Beneath a sun that loves to smile,
We'll travel far, for a little while.

The adventures start with each sweet bite,
A dance of flavors that feel so right.
With every munch, a silly sound,
As I skip and trip on fruit-filled ground!

A stretch too far, my belly's round,
It rumbles loud, oh what a sound!
With giggles loud, we try to race,
To see who finds the juiciest space!

I'll win the crown, I'm taking bets,
For nothing can beat these fruity sets.
With each delight, my heart will sing,
On juicy journeys, we'll dance and swing!

Lush Landscapes of Flavor

In a land where softness reigns supreme,
Lush landscapes sway and brightly gleam.
The fruits, they argue, 'Who's the best?'
In this juicy joke, I'm quite blessed!

I sneak a bite, oh, what a thrill,
As laughter tumbles down the hill.
The giggles mix with fruity zest,
We toast to each, for they're the best!

With every crunch, a story's spun,
Of juicy fun and endless sun.
In thick green shades, I laugh and roll,
For all sweet journeys touch the soul!

So bring your joy, your friends, your cheer,
In this flavored land, happiness is near.
A blissful league of fruity friends,
In lush landscapes, the fun never ends!

Golden Elixirs

A fruit of gold hangs up so high,
Winks at me with a cheeky eye.
Sneaky squirrels, they plot and scheme,
To taste the nectar, it seems a dream.

Juicy drips, oh what a mess,
Sticky fingers, I must confess.
With every bite, the laughter swells,
In the orchard, pure joy dwells.

The juice runs down like sunshine bright,
In fruity battles, there's no respite.
Friends gather round with grins so wide,
A zesty frolic, can't let it slide!

Golden elixirs, nature's delight,
Chasing shadows in the fading light.
With giggles and glee, we all partake,
In this merry feast, there's no mistake!

Summer's Sweet Duet

Two fruits dance in a sunny ray,
Spinning tales with every sway.
A fruity jig, oh what a sight,
In the summer's heat, it feels so right.

Laughter echoes through the trees,
As everyone munches with such ease.
A sip of juice with a splash of fun,
A sticky challenge, can't be outdone!

Fingers stained with golden cheer,
A bit too much, but never fear.
The more we eat, the more we grin,
In this festival, we all take a win!

With every bite, a joke is found,
Summer's sweet duet is all around.
In fruity harmony, we sing and shout,
Who knew joy could be this stout?

Tropical Dreams in Bloom

Bright hues splash beneath the sun,
In a garden where we laugh and run.
Each golden orb a playful tease,
In tropical bliss, we find our ease.

Children giggle, sticky and sweet,
Chasing shadows with bare feet.
A splash of juice, a squirt of fun,
In this fruity race, we all have won!

Giggling under palm tree shade,
Every bright moment we won't trade.
With slices shared and smiles wide,
In this paradise, all dreams collide.

Tropical dreams, let laughter bloom,
A symphony of joy from every room.
In the orchard's heart, let spirits soar,
Come join the fun, who could ask for more?

Euphoria of the Orchard

Beneath the boughs, the laughter floats,
With silly antics and jolly quotes.
A fruit fight here, a splashy fling,
In this orchard, we dance and sing.

The juicy goodness, oh what a thrill,
Comes with giggles and laughter still.
Beneath the trees, we take our stand,
Fruit-stained faces, all so grand!

With every munch, a story spins,
In this orchard, everyone's wins.
A splash of yellow, a burst of cheer,
We revel in this atmosphere!

Euphoria blooms in every bite,
Friends and fruit, what pure delight!
So swing by here for some silly cheer,
In the orchard's joy, we'll all appear!

Orchard Dreams Unraveled

In the orchard, chaos reigns,
Fruits are falling like soft rains.
Laughter echoes through the leaves,
As squirrels plot their sweet heists, oh please!

Baskets spill, a fruit parade,
While birds join in the charade.
Underneath the twinkling sun,
Who knew this ripeness could be such fun?

Hives of bees buzz with delight,
Chasing shadows in the light.
Sweet sticky juice drips like gold,
Each bite a story to be told!

And as we munch with great intent,
We laugh at each accidental dent.
For in this orchard, pure and wild,
We're just like kids, joyously riled!

Summer's Sweet Serenade

The sun is high, and so are we,
On a picnic blanket by the tree.
Slices glisten, a juicy show,
Sticky fingers, let it flow!

Lizards leap, and kids unite,
With laughter echoing, such delight.
A dance of fruit, a wild romance,
In this sunny, sweet expanse.

Flip-flops flying, the chase ensues,
For the last piece, it's all the news!
In a battle of giggles and zest,
The ripest fruit stands out from the rest.

Naps are missed, but who would care?
Juicy bites and sun-kissed air.
With every munch, our spirits rise,
In summer's warmth, we're all so wise!

Nectar of the Tropics

Tropical breeze and giggles blend,
Under palm trees, laughs ascend.
A splash of juice here and there,
As we run without a care!

Sun-kissed cheeks and sticky toes,
In this paradise, who knows?
Each bite's a burst, a flavor fight,
Everyone's dancing in pure delight!

With every trip, we share the tease,
Guess who's got the biggest squeeze?
Our glasses clink, a fruity cheer,
In this joy, we disappear.

A feast of colors on display,
Fun and laughter lead the way.
In this sweet paradise, we dwell,
Each juicy moment casts a spell!

A Slice of Sunshine

I found a treasure on my plate,
Sunshine slices, oh so great!
Giggles shared with every bite,
Juicy tales in morning light.

Kids in hats, they stomp and cheer,
For the fruit that draws them near.
A sticky face, a giggling laugh,
This slice of joy is our best craft!

Serenade of flavors, bright and bold,
In this funny scene, stories unfold.
We toast with cups of fruity fun,
In laughter and joy, we're never done!

So grab a slice and take a seat,
Every moment's a special treat.
In this sunshine, spirits soar,
With friendships sweet, we crave for more!

Citrus and Spice

In the market, fruits collide,
Yellow globes of joy abide.
They dance and roll, a funny sight,
Pits and peels take off in flight.

A citrus twist, so bold and bright,
Slip and slide with sheer delight.
Juice that drips on noses wide,
Oh, the giggles we cannot hide.

Skins so smooth, they tease and shout,
Bouncing here, there, about.
Lemon laughs, and lime joins in,
As they plot their fruity spin.

The Allure of Lush Fruit

Round and plump, oh what a tease,
A fruit that's sure to make us sneeze.
With every bite, a juicy mess,
Sticky fingers bring such bliss!

A taste explosion on the tongue,
Songs of sweetness barely sung.
Fruit that giggles as we chew,
Nature's candy, fresh and new.

Careful now, don't take a spill,
Slipping on juice could thrill!
The chase is on, we all take flight,
Fruits unite for a lively bite.

Summer's Succulent Symphony

In the sun, they start to sway,
Fruits turn ripe, they love to play.
Bouncing children, laughter loud,
Chasing puddles in a crowd.

Splat! A fruit hits the ground,
Everyone bursts into sound.
A ball of juice, a sweet surprise,
Sticky faces, gleeful eyes.

Colors clash, a rainbow feast,
Every bite, a wild beast.
Taste the summer, nothing shy,
Fruits are laughing, oh my, my!

Orchards in the Sky

High above, the fruits do dream,
Floating down on a sunlit beam.
With every drop, they change their shade,
A fruity circus, a grand parade.

Grab a rib or take a bite,
Fruits are soaring with delight.
In the clouds, they giggle still,
A fruity journey, what a thrill!

A piquant taste, a wild fray,
They float along, come out and play.
Laughter echoes, fruits align,
Join the fun, it's snack time!

A Festival of Flavors

Beneath the tree, our party grows,
With yellow gems and sticky toes.
Each bite a laugh, a wild delight,
As juice drips down, oh what a sight!

We juggle fruit with all our might,
And tour the yard, what a silly sight!
The dogs all dance in the sticky sun,
While we declare, 'This fruit is fun!'

Echoes of the Tropics

A sunlit dance, the colors burst,
In every dish, our taste buds thirst.
The laughter bubbles, fruity cheer,
Each scoop a joy, let's all draw near!

We build a feast, a colorful mound,
Rich aromas swirl, a joy unbound.
The party's here, the fruit's in hand,
A silly joy from this sunny land!

Sweet Laughter Under the Sun

Under bright skies, we gather round,
With giggles and laughter as our sound.
The sweet aroma twirls so high,
While sticky hands wave at the sky.

With funny hats, we play and sing,
As fruit flies by on a wild swing.
The sun smiles down, the fun won't cease,
In this crazy feast, we find our peace!

The Art of Ripeness

In twilight hues, the fruits parade,
A canvas bright, a strange charade.
We paint our faces with all the goo,
While laughing hard, what else to do?

With every bite, an artful sound,
A squishy mess on shaky ground.
The taste of fun is all around,
As we embrace this silly mound!

Sweetness on the Breeze

In a tree, high and bright,
A golden fruit, a silly sight.
Squirrels dance, they cheer and sing,
Chasing sweetness, it's a wild fling.

Ripe and juicy, drips like rain,
Sticky fingers, oh what a gain!
Happiness wrapped in a peel,
Taste so good, it's hard to conceal.

Laughter echoes through the grove,
Each slip and slide, a tale to strove.
With every bite, a giggle pops,
In this orchard, joy never stops.

So grab a slice, let worries flee,
Enjoy the fun, just you and me.
In the breeze, let sweetness tease,
Under laughter, we feel at ease.

Sunkissed Delights

On sunny days, we roam the fields,
With fruity dreams, the laughter yields.
Wobbling jars of bright delight,
Sipping sunshine, oh what a sight!

Fingers sticky, grins so wide,
A yellow feast, our joy can't hide.
Bouncing kids with faces smeared,
Their giggles loud, no one has feared.

Splatters flying, oh what a game,
Tasting sweetness, never the same.
Clouds of laughter drift so high,
As fruit flies daringly zoom by.

So join the fun, come take a bite,
A fruity wonder, pure delight.
In the sun, let laughter ring,
As cheerful hearts to joy we cling.

Whispers of the Orchard

In the orchard, stories twirl,
As fruits drop down to dance and swirl.
Critters giggle, taking their chance,
To join the joyful, crazy dance.

Bouncing fruits with every tease,
Rolling nuts down gentle breeze.
Spills and thrills, oh what a sight,
With every tumble, pure delight.

Whispers dance through leaves above,
Tales of sweetness, tales of love.
In this place, where joy takes flight,
A splash of fun, both day and night.

So come and join the silly crew,
With laughter sweet, our spirits flew.
In every whisper, joy confides,
As the orchard's heart, forever bides.

Tropical Tango

In the tropics, colors bright,
Fruits are dancing, oh what a sight!
Shake your hips, the rhythm flows,
Funky fruits in wiggly rows.

Bumpy skins and juicy treats,
Flavors bursting, oh what feats!
Grab a partner, twirl around,
In this fruity fiesta, joy abounds.

Slides and slips, we move with zest,
Laughter soars, we're truly blessed.
With every bite, the fun ignites,
In our hearts, pure delight lights.

So swing along, let worries fade,
In this vibrant, fruity parade.
Join the dance, don't miss the show,
Where fruity madness steals the glow.

The Orchard's Secret

In the garden, oh what fun,
Fruits are falling, one by one.
Squirrels giggle, chasing fast,
Who will munch their prize at last?

Sticky fingers, smiling wide,
A juicy slip, the tasty ride.
Laughter echoes, fruit-stained clothes,
Secrets whispered to the rows.

Underneath the bright sun's glow,
Dancing shadows put on a show.
With friends around, the laughter flows,
Who knew fruit could spark such prose?

In this orchard, chaos reigns,
Sweet mischief courses through the veins.
Nature's candy gives a thrill,
The secret's out, we've time to kill!

Tropical Temptations

A fruity feast, we found today,
In the sun, we laugh and play.
With sticky cheeks and juice-filled grins,
Let the tropical fun begin!

Pineapple hats and coconut shells,
A fresh concoction, the taste compels.
We're laughing loud, with hearts so light,
In this paradise, all feels right.

While the sun plays peek-a-boo,
We juggle fruits; oh, what a view!
A splash of color, a zesty cheer,
Let's toss some fruit and drink some beer!

In this bliss, we take a break,
With every bite, we're wide awake.
A party vibe, no cares allowed,
In the tropical shade, we are so proud!

Golden Tropics in Chaos

Golden globes in a leafy mess,
Rolling down, creating stress.
Watch them bounce, a wild chase,
Finding fruit in every space.

A fruity frisbee, oh what fun!
Laughs erupt beneath the sun.
Sticky hands and wild-eyed thrills,
Chasing gold like playful swills.

Pineapples roll, bananas fly,
In this chaos, we still comply.
Laughter rings through the summer air,
Who knew fruit could become this fair?

When evening falls, we'll gather all,
Share our stories, big and small.
In this madness, together we find,
A golden treasure that's one of a kind!

Sweet Tango of Summer

Come dance, my friends, it's time to sway,
With sweet fruits in vibrant display.
From juicy bites to zesty twirls,
In summer's heat, our laughter unfurls.

A tango here, a cha-cha there,
Fruit juices fly through the warm air.
Slip and slide on this juicy floor,
Every nibble, we crave for more!

Mangoes leap and coconuts spin,
In this dance, let the fun begin.
With every beat and every slice,
Sweetness wraps us like a vice!

So let's keep dancing, let's keep grin,
In this summer's sweet brimming bin.
With laughter loud and moments bright,
We'll savor fruit until the night!

The Fruit That Danced

In a grove where the laughter gleams,
A fruit spins round in joyful dreams.
It twirls and leaps, a vibrant sight,
Dressed in gold, so pure, so bright.

With every bite, a silly grin,
Juices drip down, let the fun begin!
It winks at you, oh what a tease,
A jolly treat that aims to please.

The wind whispers sweet, a playful breeze,
As fruity dancers sway with ease.
In this wild and zesty affair,
Laughter and flavor fill the air.

So join the dance, don't be shy,
With fruity revelry soaring high.
In every chuckle, and every taste,
This fruity party's never a waste.

Rhapsody of Golden Delight

A sunny day with mischief afloat,
Golden orbs in a row, oh what a joke!
They roll and bounce, a lively crew,
    As giggles echo 'round the view.

With each slice, a burst of cheer,
Those juicy globs bring us near.
Sticky fingers and smiles so wide,
    In this melody, we all confide.

A serenade of laughter rings,
As fruit flies off on curious wings.
Dancing around in a fruity ballet,
This golden song will lead the way.

So take a bite, let happiness grow,
In this rhapsody of flavors aglow.
With every chuckle, and every bite,
    We celebrate the joys of the light.

Elixirs of Summer's Serenade

Oh, summer's here, and what do you know?
Bubbly orbs in a fruity show.
Sipping sweet nectar, a delightful spree,
Kicks off the belly laughs with glee.

With giggles shared, we pass the bowl,
Each fruit a potion, tickling the soul.
In sticky chaos, the juice flies high,
Sip after sip, we're floating by.

A splash of sunshine in every taste,
Summer's elixir that none can waste.
As we gather round with a munch and a crunch,
Bursting with laughter with each chomp and punch.

In fruity tunes, we find our beat,
Every bite becomes a sweet treat.
So let's toast together, raise a cheer,
To these elixirs we hold dear.

A Festival of Colorful Abundance

In a market bright with colors galore,
Fruits line the stalls, who could ask for more?
With laughter spilling all around,
Each vibrant hue, pure joy is found.

Mashed or sliced, they spread delight,
Giggling children take their first bite.
A fruity feast, what a sight to see,
Bringing together both you and me.

Beneath the sun, where flavors clash,
Who knew fruit could be such a smash?
A carnival of colors, fun to embrace,
In every nibble, we find our place.

So let's gather close, let voices lift,
In this jam of joy, we share the gift.
With every laugh, and every cheer,
This colorful festival brings us near.

Harvesting Happiness

In the orchard, we all gather,
Laughter grows like fruits that shatter.
Buckets full of golden cheer,
Juicy bites bring everyone near.

A splat on the face, oh what a sight,
Fruit fights make the day feel bright.
Sticky fingers and sticky hair,
Who knew joy could be so rare?

We dance under the sun's warm gaze,
Chasing shadows in playful daze.
With every pluck, our spirits rise,
Harvests bring laughter, oh sweet surprise!

Days turn golden, skies blue and clear,
In fruity bliss, we hold dear.
For happiness is like this delight,
Savoring joy, with all our might.

Zest for Life

Woke up with a grin, ready to peel,
Life is juicy, it's the real deal!
Squeeze out the laughter, let it flow,
In every bite, happiness will glow.

Oranges might frown, but lemons are glee,
Our zesty crew, there's more than we see.
With every zing, we dance around,
Puns and giggles, our favorite sound!

Slicing the fruit, juice flies everywhere,
But who really cares when laughter's in the air?
Roll in the zest, do a crazy twist,
Life is too short, it's bliss that we insist!

From sun-kissed mornings to breezy nights,
We chase flavors and chase delights.
For every citrus smile we make,
Is a story, a giggle, another mistake!

The Scent of Summer

Breezes blow with a fruity scent,
Summer whispers, oh what a blend!
Picnic baskets filled to the brim,
A curious feast on the grass, a whim.

Watermelons roll, with a splat, they bounce,
Under the sun, we laugh and pounce.
A splash of juice right on our nose,
A messy delight, as our fun grows!

We crunch and munch, with joy in our hearts,
Dreaming of days where summer never departs.
A slice shared, makes friendships sweet,
With laughter and love, life's truly a treat!

Scent of peaches in the bustling air,
Every bite's an adventure, a tasty affair.
Let's savor summer, as it comes our way,
In every fruity hug, we find our play!

Rhapsody of Ripe Bliss

Ripe treasures hang from leafy vines,
Singing songs of fruity designs.
Nature's laughter in every bite,
A pop of flavor, pure delight!

Bouncing about like excited kids,
Spilling secrets and fruity bids.
With every nibble, joy ignites,
In a symphony of funny bites!

Baskets overflow, groans of elation,
Each juicy scoop, a celebration.
Sprinkled with laughter, joy takes flight,
With the sweetness of dreams, we all unite!

Days of sunshine, laughter galore,
Catching memories, we keep wanting more.
For in this dance of ripe, lush cheer,
Life is the joy we hold so dear!

The Orchard's Whimsical Dance

In a grove where the sunlight beams,
Fruits dangle like dreams in wild schemes,
With laughter that tickles the buzzing bees,
And jests of the breeze rustle through trees.

The branches sway in a cheerful blur,
As giggles of children begin to stir,
A fruit fight erupts, oh what a sight,
With sticky hands and faces so bright!

The ripe ones tumble, rolling on ground,
While everyone joins the joyous sound,
Voices ring out, echoing delight,
In this orchard, all feels just right.

As the sun sets low, painting the sky,
We savor the vibes, no need to be shy,
With each shared laugh, we become a crew,
In the orchard dance, where dreams come true.

Juicy Reveries Under Sunlight

Under a sun that gleams and grins,
We lay on grass, where fun begins,
Chasing the taste that makes us gleeful,
In juicy bites, we find it peaceful.

With cheeks as flushed as the fruit we crave,
We dive in deep, oh how we rave,
Laughter echoes with fruity delight,
Sticky stories are born tonight!

A fruit salad tower, wobbling high,
Once it's balanced, we cheer and sigh,
Then whoosh! It topples, a sugary splat,
And laughter erupts, 'Oh, imagine that!'

As dusk approaches, we dance with glee,
Twirling and swirling, so wild and free,
In golden reflection, we find our bliss,
Under the sun, we can't help but miss.

Ripe Dreams and Sticky Fingers

In a garden full of vibrant hues,
Where nature's sweetness ignites our muse,
Fingers sticky, faces smeared,
With each juicy bite, all worry disappeared.

We climb the trees for a fruit-filled thrill,
Cackles of joy, we savor the chill,
As we juggle the fruit while squealing in fun,
Who knew a snack could make us run?

Dropping our bounty with playful flair,
It splats on ground, but none of us care,
For in this chaos, we find our game,
Sticky and messy, but none feel shame!

As the sun dips low, we hug and cheer,
A memory stitched, our laughter clear,
In dreams of sweetness that linger still,
With each juicy moment, we savor the thrill.

A Symphony of Flavorful Surprises

In the orchards where laughter sings,
Surprises bloom like colorful flings,
With giggles spun from ripe delight,
And fruity treasures that feel just right.

Each bite, a note in a fruity song,
We dance to rhythms that can't go wrong,
With grins as bright as the sun's warm rays,
We celebrate joy in a thousand ways!

A fruit band plays on the picnic spread,
Bananas and berries, a feast ahead,
As silly tunes echo through the air,
We proclaim our love for this fruity affair!

With every peel and punctured skin,
We laugh together, let the fun begin,
This playful feast, forever to treasure,
In our hearts, we'll keep this sweet measure.

Chasing Ripeness

In the sun, they shine so bright,
Ripe and juicy, quite the sight.
I chase them up, I chase them down,
In fruit-filled dreams, I start to drown.

The neighbors laugh, they call me mad,
But oh, the joy! It makes me glad.
With sticky hands, I scale the wall,
For just one fruit, I'll risk it all.

Slipping here, and slipping there,
It's like a dance, out in the air.
I peep and poke, they dodge and weave,
Who knew that fruit could make me grieve?

At last, I catch one in my grip,
Then down I go—oh, what a trip!
With every bite, my heart sings loud,
For this sweet fruit, I'm feeling proud.

The Lushness of Desire

Bright orbs hang from the lofty trees,
Whispers sweetly on the breeze.
Golden glimmers full of cheer,
The luscious fruits are drawing near.

I plot and plan, a stealthy scheme,
For each ripe orb, I'll get my dream.
Like squirrels on a secret quest,
In juicy whims, I am obsessed.

The neighbors join, it's now a spree,
Who can grab the most for free?
With laughter loud, we leap and dive,
In this ripe hunt, we're all alive!

But slippery skins lead us to pounce,
And with a squish, we start to bounce.
Our laughter echoes, fills the air,
With every slip, we just don't care!

Dancer of the Palm Trees

Oh, the fruit so high, I swing with glee,
Underneath the palm tree canopy.
I shimmy up, the breeze so fine,
In the dance of fruit, I intertwine.

The coconuts watch with jealous eyes,
While silly me, I climb the skies.
With each small leap, I twist and twirl,
The leaves turn green as visions swirl.

Fruits laugh at me from their lofty thrones,
As I pluck them gently with funny groans.
Each drop that falls, a prize for all,
One little slip, and down I sprawl!

But joy persists in fruit-filled chase,
With every bite, I find my place.
No fault in laughter, pure delight,
In this crazy dance, I take flight.

Golden Drops of Joy

Rain or shine, the hunt goes on,
Underneath the glowing dawn.
Golden spheres, they call my name,
This fruity quest is quite the game.

I dodge the bees, I dance around,
Hopping, skipping on the ground.
With every splash, a juice-filled cheer,
I'm dripping sweet, oh what a smear!

My friends all join, a merry crew,
We sing and laugh, with silly who.
The world is bright, a fruity show,
The sweetest drops make spirits glow.

But fruit so ripe can lead to woe,
When every bounce becomes a throw.
Yet through the mess, we find our way,
Chasing joy in sunlit play.

A Journey in Fruit

In a land where fruits all play,
The silly citrus rolls away.
Grapes wear hats and dance on hills,
While bananas slip on joyful spills.

The cherries giggle, red and round,
Tickling the kiwi on the ground.
Peaches toss their fuzzy hair,
As laughter echoes through the air.

Pineapples join the jolly song,
With prickly crowns, they dance along.
Together they spin, excited, loud,
Creating fun, a fruity crowd!

So come along, don't miss the fun,
In this realm where all are one.
A journey sweet, a tasty quest,
In this fruit fiesta, we are blessed!

Fruitful Whirlwind

There's a whirlwind in the grove,
Where lemons dance while limes behove.
Berries tumble, in spirals they whiz,
This fruit fest is the craziest biz!

Pears provide the witty banter,
As coconuts become the dancer.
A fruity twirl, oh what a sight,
With a splash of juice, pure delight!

Oranges giggle, citrusy bright,
While plums spin round with all their might.
Tropical fun, it never ends,
Join the chaos, make new friends!

In this happenstance fruit-filled spree,
Be ready for laughs and wild glee.
A whirlwind of flavors spins us 'round,
In this juicy joy, we are unbound!

Sweet Ecstasy of the Tropics

In tropics where the sun shines bright,
Fruits party hard, what a sight!
Coconuts wear their beachy swag,
While lemons put on a cheerful drag.

Pineapples prance in the warm, warm sun,
With happy hearts, they have pure fun.
Papayas leap, so very bold,
A sweet ecstasy, a story told!

Passion fruits giggle, full of cheer,
In laughter, they make the world clear.
Bananas slip in a playful race,
With fruity joy lighting up the place!

So join this chase of tropical mirth,
Where laughter bounces, oh what a berth!
Every fruit here sings a tune,
In the sweet ecstasy, under the moon!

Harvesting Radiance

In fields of gold, the fruits await,
Where laughter bursts from every crate.
Harvesting smiles, bright and true,
Bananas beam in the morning dew.

Bright berries boast their shiny coats,
While apples sing with silly notes.
In this place of fruitful dreams,
Radiance bursts at the seams!

Gathering joy, all hands are keen,
As fruits play tricks, oh what a scene!
Tangerines juggle, whole and pure,
A harvest party, that's for sure!

So let us gather, sing aloud,
In this bustling, fruity crowd.
With every bite, we'll share delight,
Harvesting radiance feels so right!

www.ingramcontent.com/pod-product-compliance
Lightning Source LLC
Chambersburg PA
CBHW050305120526
44590CB00016B/2497